a guide to
meditation

Lorraine Turner

𝑝

This is a Parragon Book

This edition published in 2002

Parragon

Queen Street House

4 Queen Street

Bath BA1 1HE, UK

ISBN: 0-75259-470-2

Printed in China

Designed and created with The Bridgewater Book Company Ltd.

NOTE

Any information given in this book is not intended to be taken
as a replacement for medical advice. Any person with a condition
requiring medical attention should consult a qualified medical
practitioner or therapist before beginning this or any
other exercise programme.

Contents

Introduction

People have used meditation for thousands of years in their quest for inner harmony. All the major religions, including Buddhism, Islam, Hinduism and Christianity, use in their teachings to help attain spiritual enlightenment. Meditation improves concentration, increases self-awareness and enables us to combat stress by helping us to relax and cope. It even helps us to get on better with others. Many people who meditate improve their physical and mental well-being, and some have been able to conquer depression or addictions to drugs, caffeine or alcohol.

The Buddha reached enlightenment through meditation and devoted the rest of his life to teaching others what he had learned.

Mind control

There is no doubt that the mind's ability to analyse, discriminate, plan and communicate has helped us reach where we are today. Yet it can be a double-edged sword. Although the brain may help us to reason, to think creatively and to relate to others, if we do not learn to switch it off it can overwhelm us. It can persecute us with fears about failure, our appearance or the opinions others may have of us. Meditation can bring relief from these anxieties by helping us to silence inner chatter, to recognise and dismiss negative thoughts, and to create a feeling of peace and serenity.

"All you need is deep within you waiting to unfold and reveal itself. All you have to do is be still and take time to seek for what is within, and you will surely find it."

EILEEN CADDY

Health and work benefits

Clinical studies into the effects of meditation are encouraging: they have shown reductions in migraines, insomnia, irritable bowel syndrome, premenstrual syndrome, anxiety and panic attacks, as well as lower levels of stress hormones, lower blood pressure and improved circulation. They have also shown that meditation can help control pulse and respiratory rates, and increase job satisfaction and work performance. As a result, doctors are now beginning to recognise the therapeutic benefits of meditation and some are already recommending meditation exercises and relaxation techniques to their patients to help treat stress-related ailments.

Meditation is for everyone, whatever their lifestyle.

Meditation for everyone

Nowadays, meditation is no longer the preserve of mystics, yogis and philosophers. Its value has been recognised by many well-known individuals and groups, including celebrities such as The Beatles, Tina Turner and Richard Gere. You don't have to be religious or have huge amounts of time to meditate – you can do it no matter how old or busy you are. So, if you want to learn how to beat stress, understand more about yourself or increase your sense of well-being, this book is for you.

We owe our advances to the power of the mind, but we need to learn how to control it.

What is meditation?

Meditation is much more than simply relaxation: during relaxation the mind wanders uncontrollably, whereas during meditation the mind stays alert and focused. By using meditation to restrain the wanderings of the mind, we can bring ourselves back to full awareness and experience things as they really are.

Practising meditation

Meditation is a time-honoured method of controlling the mind and there are many different ways to do it. In fact, there are literally thousands of different meditation exercises. Many of them have one thing in common – they start with a period of relaxation, then the mind is given one point of focus and concentrates on this and nothing else. Every time the mind tries to stray onto something else, it is gently but firmly brought back to the point of focus.

Many people find this difficult to do at first, especially if they have been used to letting their minds wander without restraint, but most people can get over this with a little practice. Even if you can only manage a couple of minutes at a time, you will soon see results if you do it regularly. It doesn't need to be hard work: meditation should be enjoyable, and if you allow yourself, say, at least five minutes a day at first, you will soon find that you look

forward to these periods and enjoy them as special times for yourself.

There are many different ways to meditate. Some call for exercises that focus on a particular object, such as a leaf or a sound.

There are all kinds of ways you can meditate and even a few minutes can make a difference to the way you feel.

Some use chanting, or withdrawal or expansion of the senses in some way. Others involve contemplation on a concept such as love, anger or growing old. You can also mix different methods and approaches. For example, you may start off by focusing on your breath, and then move on to contemplate the nature of friendship.

Restoring balance

Meditation helps us to restore balance between the left and right sides of the brain. The left side of the brain deals with thinking, speaking and writing. When we are awake and in a busy, thinking state of mind, the brain emits faster electrical patterns called 'beta' waves. In this state we are able to rationalise and think about the past and future.

The right side of the brain deals with intuition, imagination and feeling. When we are sensing something – such as listening to music – and we are in a receptive rather than an active state, the brain emits slower electrical patterns called 'alpha' waves. In the alpha state we are more passive and open to our feelings. The alpha state is most likely to happen when we let ourselves live in the present rather than in the future or the past. It often happens just before or after sleep (but not during sleep – when we are sleeping the brain emits other waves, called theta and delta).

When we are awake we are usually in beta most of the time, and spend only about an hour in the alpha state. Meditation helps to restore the balance by increasing our time spent in alpha: it helps us to recover feeling and to experience the world directly, in the present, before the sensations become 'interpreted' by the left side of the brain.

Alpha	Beta
Receptive	Active
Intuition	Thought
Present	Past/future
Relaxed	Tense
Being	Doing
Listening	Talking
Imagination	Calculation

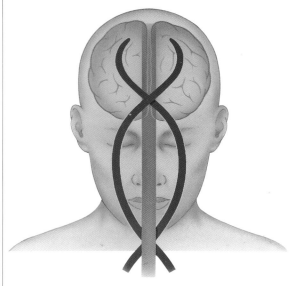

Meditation can create better balance between the thinking and emotional sides of the brain.

Finding time to meditate

If you lead a very busy life, you may be wondering how you are going to fit in enough time for regular meditation. Many of us have work and family commitments, but often all that is needed is a little planning and reorganisation to help you incorporate meditation into your daily life. After a while, it will become a habit.

Meditating regularly

When the word 'meditation' is mentioned, some people automatically think of ascetic hermits and monks spending days in a trance-like state in isolated caves and temples. Although some very dedicated practitioners of meditation do spend their time like that, for the majority of people there is no need to go to such extremes. You only need to meditate for a few minutes at a time, but in order to make steady and noticeable progress you should try to meditate regularly.

Effective time management

If your life is hectic and full of commitments, you may not find it easy to think about having to fit in something else, but it may help if you look on this one as a commitment to yourself. Your meditation periods are going to be times that you can spend entirely on yourself, which is a very good reason for finding the time to do it. After all, everyone is entitled to spare at least a few minutes each day for themselves.

Managing your time more effectively will have other benefits too. You may find that you are more organised and have less pressures and more leisure time. This will help you to be more relaxed and therefore better able to concentrate on your meditation, which in turn will help you to feel calmer, too.

A busy life is no barrier to practising meditation; all you need is a few minutes.

Writing down a timetable of your week may help you to pinpoint times for meditation.

Saving time

Making time for meditation needn't be difficult. Start by drawing up a timetable for yourself: it doesn't have to be exact, just a timetable of a typical week laid out on a piece of paper. List all the things you normally do on a regular basis, such as going to work (include travelling time), taking the kids to school or doing the shopping on a Saturday afternoon. Decide roughly what time you go to bed each evening, and block out time for that.

When you have got all the regular events down on paper, make a list of tasks that you should do regularly but may sometimes miss. These could include weeding the garden, for example, or filing your bills and letters. Allocate enough time for these jobs. Since they may vary from week to week, you may want to allow two or three hours at a certain

time each week to catch up on these tasks before they get out of hand. After you have done this, take another look at your timetable.

You may be surprised at how much more time there is than you originally thought. Now you have to find out where the rest of the time is being spent. Perhaps you have been spending more time watching TV than you realised, for instance, or doing things for other people that they could quite easily do for themselves. If you find you have plenty of blank spaces in your timetable but can't account for them, you may find it helpful to keep a diary of all your activities for a week, and note carefully how much time you have spent on each one. You may find that the shopping actually takes you twice as long as you thought, or that you forgot to include a regular task in your schedule. A diary will help you to spot these things, and to plug the holes in your timetable.

Allocating yourself enough time for chores can make them seem more pleasurable.

Making priorities and delegating tasks

Now it is time to make a list of all the one-off jobs you have been meaning to do, but haven't found the time for yet, such as painting the front door, calling a relative, or oiling that squeaky hinge. Include everything, no matter how small. Then prioritise them by giving them numbers. For example, you could allot number 1 to the most urgent task, then number 2 to the next most urgent job, and so on. Now go back to your timetable, and allocate a period of time each week to clearing these tasks. Tick them off as you do them, and add any new ones to the list as they arise. Renumber them when necessary.

When you have done this, study your timetable and see what time you have left. Very likely you will have some

Free up some time to spend on yourself.

Learn to delegate and give everyone in the household specific tasks to do.

spare slots for meditation, but if your timetable is still packed, then you should look carefully at what is using up all your time. If it is work, then do another timetable for work and prioritise all your tasks within it. If you still can't fit them all in, then you will have identified a problem: you are overworked! If this is the case, you should take steps to ease the situation: get help and delegate any tasks you don't need to do yourself.

If you are spending too much time doing housework or looking after other people when they are capable of doing things themselves, ask for help here too. Sometimes all that is needed is a simple request to spur people into action. If your requests are ignored, however, you may have to be firm!

Other time-savers

Changing a few of your everyday habits can often save a lot of time during the day. Try some of these simple techniques and see how much time you can save:

- Open your mail over the wastepaper basket, and bin unnecessary items immediately.

- Answer letters the day they come in.

- File things away as you deal with them.

- Control the amount of time you spend on the telephone. If someone you know is a chatterbox, try calling at times when you know you can keep the call short, such as just before that person's favourite TV programme. Your telephone bill and your timetable will love you for it!

- Limit your time spent watching TV: choose the programmes you particularly want to watch, and then switch off the TV when you have finished watching.

- Be vigilant about people offloading jobs onto you. For example, if someone says to you 'can you ring so and so', explain that you haven't got time and suggest that he or she makes the phone call instead.

These are just some of the ways by which you can make more time in your life to meditate. There are many, many more. Try some of the suggestions straight away, so that you can start planning in your meditation times and enjoy the benefits that regular practice can bring.

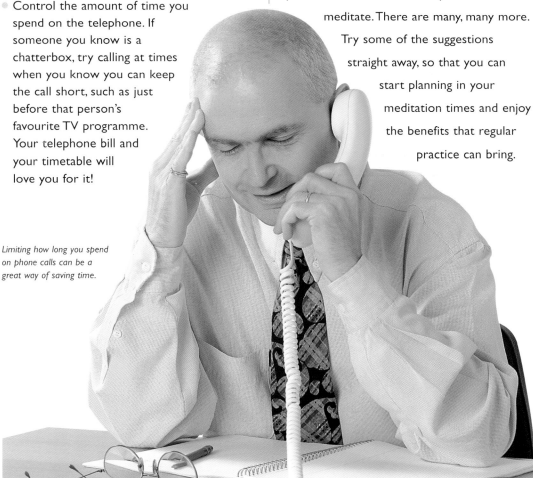

Limiting how long you spend on phone calls can be a great way of saving time.

Preparing to meditate

In an ideal world, we would each have a special place for meditation: a quiet sanctuary where, as soon as we enter it, everyday stresses melt away and we are instantly in the mood for meditation. In reality, however, most of us do not have the luxury of such a place; we may not even be able to choose where we meditate at any given time.

Creating a space for meditation

If you do not have a spare room at home that you can devote to meditation, there may be a corner or a peaceful spot in a quiet room that you can reserve for the purpose. If you keep this spot just for meditation, your brain will associate it with peaceful feelings and instantly put you in the right state of mind whenever you go there. Don't worry if that's not possible though. You can still create the right atmosphere by adding a special chair, or by keeping some tranquil sounds on hand, such as classical music. Don't meditate in bed because it is easy to fall asleep.

Learning to improvise

If you do not have a quiet space in your home where you can meditate regularly, don't worry. There are many other places you can try – all it takes is a little improvisation. For example, if the weather is dry, why not go to your local park? Find a bench, or sit with your back to a tree, or sit on the grass in a quiet spot. If it is raining, there may be a gazebo or other small shelter that you can use.

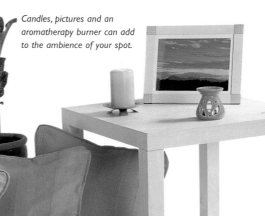

Candles, pictures and an aromatherapy burner can add to the ambience of your spot.

If you are lucky enough to live near beautiful scenery, you have the ideal meditation area.

The most important thing is to find a quiet spot where you will not be interrupted, even if this turns out to be a quiet nook in a city street. If the weather is bad, try your local library, a church, or even your car.

To create a good atmosphere, try listening to some peaceful music through headphones before you start and after you have finished, for example, or carry something with you, such as a flower or other inspiring object.

Your clothes should be comfortable and loose. Take some extra clothing if you are going to be outside: you feel the cold more if you sit in the same position for any length of time.

Spontaneity

Although it helps to choose a suitable spot and create the right atmosphere before you meditate, there may be times when you suddenly feel like meditating wherever you are, without any preparation at all. For example, you may suddenly feel like meditating on a train or on a bus. This is fine, and as you will see later in this book, as your concentration improves, you will find that you can meditate anywhere, even in the most crowded of situations.

Listening to tranquil music can help you to relax and prepare for meditation.

Posture and breathing

Correct posture and breathing are essential for good meditation practice, but you don't have to torture yourself with difficult yoga stances and complicated breathing sequences. Meditation should be enjoyable, so make sure you are comfortable so that you can meditate, uninterrupted, for any length of time.

Basic postures

There are many different meditation postures to choose from, but you only need to concentrate on the ones given here.

Seated posture

You can use a chair, stool or bench for this posture. Sit up, with your back straight. Hold your head and spine in alignment. Rest your hands comfortably on your knees, or on the arms of the chair. Your thighs should be parallel to the floor. If you are using a chair, make sure you do not lean against the back of it.

You may prefer to sit on a chair rather than the floor, but make sure you sit up straight.

Cross-legged posture

Sit on the floor and cross your legs. There is no need to raise your feet and rest them on your thighs the way the Indian yogis do – in fact you should avoid it unless you are skilled at yoga. Simply sit on the floor and cross your legs, feet tucked under your legs. Sit upright, back straight and your head and spine in alignment. Rest your hands on your knees. Sit cross-legged on a cushion if you find it more comfortable.

Take a little time to find a comfortable position before starting.

Kneeling posture

Kneel on the floor, knees together, buttocks on your heels and toes almost touching. Keep your back straight, head and spine in alignment, and rest your palms on your thighs. Put a cushion on the backs of your heels and rest on this if you find it comfortable.

Kneeling position

Lying down posture

This is known as Savasana, or the 'corpse' posture in yoga. Simply lie down on your back on a carpeted floor or rug. Your legs should be straight but relaxed. Let your arms rest comfortably by your sides. The lying down posture is not ideal for meditation because it is much easier to fall asleep in it. However, it can be useful if you are feeling particularly stressed and need to relax (see page 17), or if you are very tired and need revitalising.

Lying down posture

Counting the breaths

This is one of the easiest and best-known meditations. Do it for as long as feels comfortable. A few minutes may be all you can manage at first, but try to build up to about 20 minutes if you can.

1 *Adopt the seated or cross-legged posture (see opposite). Close your eyes, relax your body and breathe normally for a few breaths.*

2 *Focus your attention on your breathing. After each exhalation, but before breathing in, count silently as follows: 'One' (inhale, exhale), 'Two' (inhale, exhale) and so on until you reach 'Five', then start again from 'One'.*

3 *Feel the air going in and out as you breathe. You will soon notice how your mind tries to distract you from counting, with all manner of thoughts. Just bring it gently back each time you realise you have been sidetracked. When you have finished, come back from the meditation slowly and open your eyes.*

Relaxation

Being able to relax is essential for meditation, but many people find it hard to do. Lifestyles today are more stressful than ever, with increasing work, family, and financial pressures taking their toll on our bodies and our peace of mind.

Effects of stress

Some stress is good for us: it motivates us to take action and can even help to save us from danger. Imagine that you are about to be attacked by a tiger, for example. The stress response, or 'fight or flight' mechanism, will kick in. Adrenaline is pumped into the system, the heart, breathing and metabolism speed up, and anti-inflammatory agents such as cortisol

A meditation or yoga class can help you to learn the skill of total relaxation.

are released. Systems not immediately essential – such as the digestive and immune systems – close down. If you then run to escape danger, the physical action releases the stress. Your body relaxes and returns to normal.

In normal life, we do not always have an outlet for stress; we can't run out of a difficult meeting, for example. Stress chemicals stay in the body, obstructing the digestive and immune systems and depleting our energy. The long-term effects of this can lead to serious illness.

Learning to relax

Relaxation is vital to good health: it helps to combat stress, and gives the body time to replenish its energy. It is also essential to relax before, during and after meditation in order to get into and maintain the alpha state (see page 7). Here are some suggestions to help you relax:

- Try unwinding in a hot bath
- Listen to some gentle music
- Have a massage
- Join a relaxation group or yoga class

Receiving a massage can be a wonderful way of relaxing tension in your body.

Relaxing the body

You can perform this exercise on its own, or before or after other meditation exercises.

1 Adopt the lying down posture (see page 15). Close your eyes and breathe naturally. Move your attention to the top of your head, and notice any tension there. Once you have located the tension, relax and let it go. Feel the gentle movement of your breathing.

2 Move your attention down to your forehead, and let any tension go from here. Relax your eyebrows and eyelids, ears, nostrils, mouth and jaw, releasing the tension as you go. Keep breathing normally.

3 Move your focus to your neck, then down through your shoulders, arms and hands. Release all the tension in those areas. Then shift your concentration to your chest and heart, stomach, abdomen, buttocks and genitals, relaxing each area as you go. Finally, move your attention to your legs and feet and remove all the tension here.

4 Breathe for a few moments. After a while you may find that tension has started to creep back into some parts of your body. If so, try to feel where the tension is located and consciously let it go again.

5 Come back from the meditation slowly and open your eyes. You will feel refreshed.

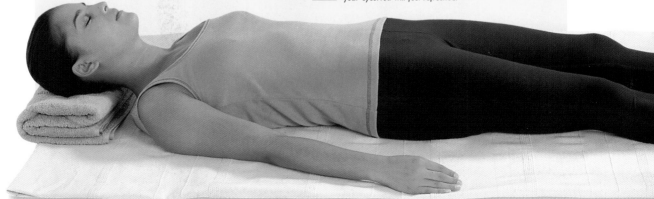

Mindfulness

Many of us spend our time 'sleepwalking'. We perform actions automatically and are unaware of what is happening around us. While we are sitting on a bus, for example, we may be thinking about the past. As a result, precious moments in the present are lost. We may not notice the scenes passing by or who is sitting next to us. Mindfulness helps us to reclaim each moment, to live in the present so that nothing passes us by.

Taking the time to be aware helps you to connect to your experience of the moment.

become fully aware in the present moment, heightens our sensitivity and enables us to perform tasks more efficiently. It also makes us more observant. For example, a doctor who listens with mindfulness to a patient will be aware of everything that is happening to the patient in the present moment – even the tiniest details – which will help the doctor to be more sensitive to that patient's needs.

Cultivating mindfulness

A certain amount of automatic activity isn't necessarily bad: it gives us time to remember things and to plan ahead. However, too much dwelling on the past or the future means that the most valuable time – the present – is lost. Cultivating mindfulness, or learning to

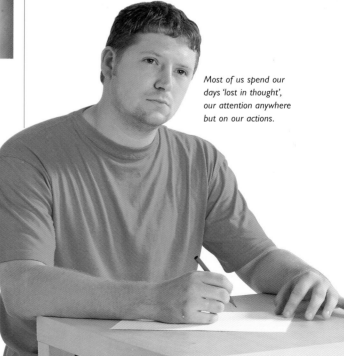

Most of us spend our days 'lost in thought', our attention anywhere but on our actions.

To develop mindfulness, you need to keep yourself totally in the present, noticing every sensation and every detail of what is going on. If you are writing a letter mindfully, for example, you will notice everything about it: the smell of the fresh sheet of paper before you start writing, the feel of the paper against the skin of your hand, the weight of the pen and how it rests between your fingers, the flow of the ink as the shapes of the letters form, even the speed of the pen's movements, and your thoughts and feelings during the process. Nothing, no matter how small, escapes your attention. You see everything, feel everything, and with a sense of peaceful detachment. You don't try to analyse or judge anything, you just watch and feel.

Living in the present

When you are truly living in the present, everything takes on a new meaning. Colours are brighter and more vivid, objects appear in striking detail, and you can hear every note in a piece of music. Flowers smell heavenly, and every sensation is intense. You can cultivate this awareness by doing the 'Mindfulness meditation'.

Bringing mindfulness to the simplest action engages your senses.

Mindfulness meditation

This meditation is excellent for cultivating mindfulness. Try to do it whenever you can.

1 *Pull your mind away from wherever it is, and concentrate on what you are doing at that moment. It doesn't matter whether you are standing up, walking, or sitting down. Whatever you are doing – walking home, eating, having a shower – start doing it with all your senses. Smell the fragrance of the air around you, taste every mouthful of food you are eating, feel the sensation of water against your skin as you shower. Ask yourself what you are doing, and what you are experiencing and feeling.*

2 *After a short while, you will probably find your mind trying to distract you. Notice the thoughts that arise, but don't follow them. Let them go, and bring your mind gently back to the present moment. You will gradually find yourself moving into the peaceful alpha state (see page 7). Keep this meditation going for as long as you can.*

Mindfulness meditation helps you to see the beauty in everything from the tiniest flower to the people closest to you.

Affirmations

Affirmations are statements that you can repeat silently or out loud to yourself, over and over, until the constant repetition becomes meaningless and you are aware only of the sound of the affirmation in your head. Although repeating statements in this way may seem pointless at first, try to persevere because they are a powerful tool and can have some very positive effects on your mind and overall well-being.

Affirmations in daily life

In everyday life, people can use affirmations to reprogramme their minds into a more positive way of thinking. Say a man has been asked to speak at a wedding. The 'chatterer within' takes over and torments him with fears about making a fool of himself. Eventually he is so tense that he can't concentrate at all.

Thinking positively can have a beneficial effect on how you feel about yourself.

The man decides to use the affirmation 'I am a good public speaker', and repeats it to himself constantly. He doesn't believe it at first but the constant repetition renders the statement meaningless and its implication doesn't jar. It starts to feel almost natural to say it, and he feels comfortable with it.

Used correctly, affirmations can help you to let go of self-doubt and embrace confidence.

Since the statement is familiar, the left side of the brain no longer needs to analyse it and it passes to the right side of the brain. The right side is not concerned with judgement, only emotion and sensation. It will accept the thought without question and transform it into a positive feeling. Fears of failure will dissipate, and a new self-confidence will emerge.

Any statement can be used as an affirmation: just make sure it gives you a good feeling, is confident in tone, and easy to say. For example:

I am very confident
I forgive myself
My body is beautiful
I am at peace
I am completely relaxed

Try writing your affirmation down, then put it in a place where you will see it often.

Affirmations can help you to see yourself in a more positive light.

Affirmations in meditation

In meditation, affirmations are often used for a different purpose, namely to stop the endless chatter of the brain. If, when you are meditating, you find it hard to stop your mind from distracting you, repeating a simple affirmation blocks the communication channel so that the mind cannot feed you other thoughts. It works in the same way as counting the breaths (see page 15) in that it enables you to block out distractions by concentrating on something else. Some people find affirmations easier to do than counting the breaths.

During meditation, we usually repeat affirmations while we are focusing on something else, such as sensations. Since the purpose of the affirmation is to block out invading thoughts, the meaning of the affirmation is unimportant, but it does no harm to choose to say something positive so that, after constant repetition, the idea will take root in the subconscious mind. However, remember that the main aim here is to counteract the chattering of the brain, not to feed it ideas that may distract you further.

Regular practice can help to get you used to affirmation work. Once you feel comfortable with it, try experimenting with other simple phrases that are meaningful to you.

Affirmations in action

The best time to repeat an affirmation is when you are relaxed. In this way, you will be better able to counteract the chatter of your mind, and the suggestion behind the affirmation will move from the realm of thought into the realm of feeling more quickly. If you are having trouble relaxing, perform the 'Relaxing the body' exercise first (see page 17). The main thing to remember with affirmations is that you should repeat them regularly. Repeat them for as long as feels comfortable, but as a guide, start with repeating them at least three times each session, three times a day.

Other affirmations

Try the 'Affirmation exercise' opposite, then try it using any other affirmations of your choice. The most suitable ones will be those that help you to counteract inner chatter; they should be easy to fit into the rhythm of your breathing. Here are some suggestions:

let it go
                peace forever
wide awake
                joyful and free

Feeling relaxed before you start your affirmations will help you to embrace them more quickly and effectively.

Affirmation exercise

This exercise is very effective for controlling the mind and improving concentration.

It is also a great stress reliever.

1 Adopt either the seated, kneeling or lying down posture (see pages 14–15). Make sure you are really relaxed before you start. If necessary, perform the 'Relaxing the body' exercise first (see page 17). Let go of any tension, allowing it to fall away from your body.

2 Bring your attention to your breathing. Breathe in and out naturally, following the rhythm of your breath rather than trying to control it.

3 When you feel ready, repeat the word 'RELAX' to yourself, either silently or out loud. Say the first syllable, 'RE', as you breathe in, and the second syllable, 'LAX' as you breathe out. Don't try to force your breathing into any particular rhythm or pattern. Just keep breathing normally and match the speed of the affirmation to your breathing.

4 You may find your mind tries to sway you with other thoughts. Just bring your mind gently back and continue to repeat the word 'RELAX' in rhythm with your breathing. Repeat it for as long as feels comfortable.

5 When you have finished the exercise, notice how you feel. You will probably be more relaxed, but note any other feelings as well.

Consciously let go of tension in each area of your body to reach a truly relaxed state.

Mantras

Mantras are similar to affirmations, in that they are statements that you can repeat to yourself. Unlike affirmations, however, the sound qualities of mantras are important, and are said to resonate through the body to bring about a transformation of consciousness. Some people believe that mantras possess magical powers.

Followers of the Buddha use the mantra Om Mani Padme Hum *to evoke compassion.*

Mantras for everyone

There is no doubt that some mantras do have a magical quality about them, and they are often found in spiritual traditions. The Hindus have used mantras for thousands of years and so have Buddhists, Muslims and Christians.

You don't have to be religious to use mantras, however. You can choose mantras that are not linked to a particular deity. Mantras can be used to induce a state of peace and tranquillity or they can be used to increase awareness, alertness or creativity.

Well-known mantras

Probably the most famous mantra of all is OM. It is Hindu in origin and is pronounced 'A-OO-M' (the 'A' is sounded like the 'a' in 'car'). Hindus believe that OM is the sound vibration that underlies the creation of the universe. It is considered a very powerful mantra and is a good one to choose if you want to identify with the Oneness of the universe and all of creation.

OM MANI PADME HUM is another well-known mantra, which is often used by Buddhists to evoke compassion and dispel negative feelings towards oneself or others. This mantra is also said to help keep you alert while you relax. It is pronounced 'AOOM-MANI-PADMAY-HOOM'.

If you are a Christian, a popular mantra to use is ALLELUIA, pronounced 'AH-LAY-LOO-YA'. It is also intoned as HALLELUIA, pronounced 'HAH-LAY-LOO-YA'. It comes from the Hebrew *hallelu* (praise) and *Jah* (Jehovah), and means 'praise God'.

Mantra exercise

You can use any mantra you like for this exercise, but it helps to choose one that has a particular resonance or special quality of sound. You may only be able to do this exercise for a few minutes at first, but try to build up to at least 20 minutes.

1 *Adopt the cross-legged posture or any other seated posture (see page 14). Close your eyes and breathe naturally.*

2 *Start repeating the mantra that you have chosen. You can repeat it silently or aloud, whichever you wish. If it helps you, try repeating it in time with the natural rhythm of your breathing or your heartbeat.*

3 *Let the rhythm and sound of the mantra take you up and carry you along. If you lose your concentration, bring your mind back gently but firmly, and try repeating the mantra with more emphasis.*

4 *Come out of the meditation slowly and open your eyes.*

The power of mantras

The mantra's sound quality, even when it exists only in thought, will still resonate through the body. You can repeat a mantra in rhythm with your breath or heartbeat, or intone it freely.

At first, it is probably better to use mantras that are known to work well. Later on, you can try creating your own. Just make sure the sound resonates and hums through your body.

Here are some suggestions:

love

peace   silence

one   doh   shhhh

oo   ahhhh   mmmm

Standing and walking meditation

Meditation can be done anywhere, at any time. You don't even have to be sitting or lying down. You can meditate while standing, walking, or even dancing.

Standing posture

Stand erect with your feet about 45 cm (18 inches) apart. Your feet should be parallel to each other, and your head and spine in alignment. Keep your pelvis straight so that your lower back does not curve inwards. Above all, don't strain. Your standing position should be comfortable so that you can maintain the posture without getting tired.

When you stand straight, but relaxed, energy can flow freely through your body.

Golden flower meditation

This meditation is excellent for developing your powers of concentration. It is also revitalising, and calls on the earth's energy instead of depleting your own.

1 *Adopt the standing posture (see left) and allow any tension to drop away from you. Breathe naturally and smoothly.*

2 *Imagine your spine as a straight stem. Feel it growing upwards, from your lower back up between your shoulders to the back of your neck. It continues up above your head until a large, golden flower blooms. The flower head travels upwards a little further, pulling your spine straighter.*

3 *At the same time, imagine your feet as the flower's roots. Feel your feet go deeper into the earth. Between the flower above your head and the roots that are your feet, feel your spine stretch out just a little more. Your arms and hands become the leaves, as light as air.*

4 *Now imagine energy, in the form of golden-white light, travelling up from the roots that are your feet, up through your spine to the top of your head, where the golden flower shines. The light fills your body with cleansing energy, and revitalises you. Hold this image for a few seconds.*

5 *Let the light descend through your body, into the earth. See the flower close, and the stem relax and become your spine again. Relax.*

Practising mindfulness while walking will make you more aware of the earth's natural beauty.

Walking with mindfulness

This meditation helps to develop concentration and increases awareness.

It is also very relaxing and enjoyable.

1 While you are out walking, perhaps to or from work or simply going for a stroll, bring your mind away from thoughts of the past or the future. Focus on your breathing and walk erect, with your head and spine in alignment.

2 Shift your attention to your walking. Walk mindfully, focusing on each step. Notice how your weight shifts from one foot to the other, the way your arms and legs move, and how the air feels on your face.

3 Now expand your awareness to include everything around you. Where are you? Who or what is there with you? Listen to the sounds, and notice the smells, colours and movements. How do you feel about this experience? Try to take in as many sensations as you can.

The chakras

In Indian yoga, chakras are great centres of energy in the body. Although they are invisible to the eye, these spinning wheels of spiritual energy keep our bodies and spirits in balance. They store the powerful life force that yogis call *prana,* the Chinese call *ch'i* and the Japanese call *ki.* This dynamic energy is the precious universal life force that permeates everything; it surrounds and is within all things.

Exploring the chakras

The seven main chakras of the body are sited between the base of the spine and the top of the head. There are other chakras, but in this book we will concentrate on those listed here.

● The first, or base, chakra is located at the base of the spine. It is associated with anything of a material nature, including physical strength and structures, possessions, status in life and survival. It is also where a dormant energy called *kundalini* is stored. Yogis aim to reactivate this energy and send it flowing through the chakras. When it reaches the top and all the chakras are open and in balance with one another, enlightenment is attained.

● The second chakra, or sacral chakra, is located at the level of the lower abdomen, above the genitals. It is associated with sexuality, sensuality and reproduction.

● The third chakra, or solar plexus chakra, is located at the solar plexus area (this is high at the back of the abdomen, just between the ribs and navel). This wheel of energy governs inner power, the will and self-confidence.

● The fourth chakra, or heart chakra, is positioned at the level of the heart. It is associated with relationships, as well as love, compassion and emotions in general.

● The fifth chakra, or throat chakra, is located in the throat area. It is concerned with expression and communication and also with our creative impulses.

● The sixth chakra, or brow chakra, is positioned at the level of the forehead, between the eyebrows. It is associated with imagination, clarity of thought, intuition and dreams, as well as our psychic abilities.

● The seventh chakra, or crown chakra, is situated on the top of the head. It governs understanding, higher consciousness and our link with universal spirit and the divine.

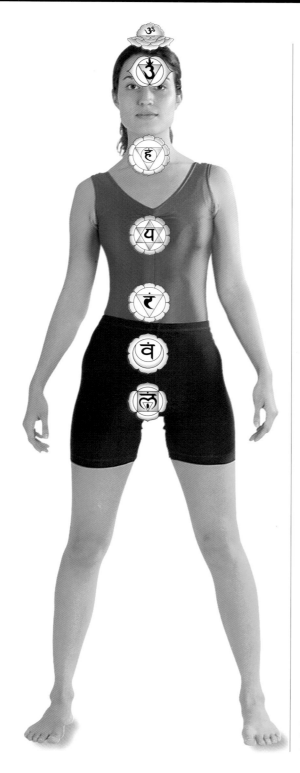

Achieving balance

An essential thing to bear in mind about the chakras is that energy should flow naturally between them and that they should be in balance with one another. Meditation can help to balance the chakras in order to ensure pure energy flow, enhance spiritual awareness and improve overall well-being.

If a particular chakra is 'blocked', it can create problems in the area with which it is associated. For example, if the second chakra is blocked, it may interfere with sexual expression or with the normal function of the reproductive system. Likewise, if the fifth chakra is blocked, it can inhibit self-expression or the flow of creativity. Very few people actually have all their chakras open and in balance and the process of attaining this state should be seen as a long-term one.

In fact, any in-depth work on opening all the chakras calls for advanced training and self-discipline and should only be done under the guidance of a suitably qualified and experienced teacher. However, if you would like to learn more about them, feel where your own chakras are or experience a little of their energy for yourself, you can do so.

The six lower chakras ascend up the body, their positions corresponding to the spinal column. The highest chakra is located at the crown.

Petals of the lotus

When meditating on one of the chakras, it is customary to imagine it as a lotus with a certain number of petals. The lotus has special significance because although its roots are in the mud, it blossoms into a beautiful flower that opens its petals to the heavens above. If you find a lotus flower difficult to imagine, you can simply visualise each chakra as a storehouse of energy. The following table gives the names and positions of the seven main chakras, together with their associated colours and number of petals.

As you work up through the chakras, you can visualise lotus flowers with open petals.

Attributes of the seven main chakras

Chakra	Indian name	Position	Attributes	Colour	Gland and body system	Number of petals
Base	Muladhara	Base of spine	Material plane, status in life, survival	Red	Adrenals, skeleton, lymph, and elimination system	4
Sacral	Swadhisthana	Lower abdomen, just above genitals	Sexuality and sensuality	Orange	Gonads and reproduction system	6
Solar plexus	Manipura	Solar plexus or navel area	Inner power, will and confidence	Yellow	Pancreas, muscles and digestive system	10
Heart	Anahata	Heart area	Relationships, as well as love, compassion, and emotions in general	Green	Thymus, respiration, circulation and immune system	12
Throat	Vishuddha	Throat	Expression, creativity and communication	Turquoise and blue	Thyroid and metabolism	16
Brow	Ajna	Between eyebrows	Imagination, clarity of thought, intuition and dreams	Indigo	Pituitary and endocrine system	2
Crown	Sahasrara	Top of head	Understanding, higher consciousness and link with the divine	Violet	Pineal and nervous system	1,000

how the chakras are positioned in the body. If you want to see the chakras as spinning circles, you would have to place yourself above the person's head and look down through the person's chakras from above. In this way, you would be able to see that the chakras are round.

It can be difficult to imagine the chakras; using a CD can help you to picture them.

Locating the chakras

Contrary to popular belief, the chakras are positioned horizontally. In other words, if you are looking at a standing person face to face, the chakras are not positioned flat against the person's body like spinning buttons. They are actually on a horizontal plane, so that you can only see them side on.

If you want to see this visually, try this experiment. Hold your index finger upright in front of your eyes. Put a CD on your finger and spin it, and you will find that you can only see the CD side on – only the edge of the CD will be visible. This is

The Sushumna channel

To make things as easy to visualise as possible, you can imagine the chakras running up your spine at the back of your body, or running up the front of your body. You can also visualise them going up inside your body between the back and the front. To be more precise, however, they actually ascend up a central channel called the *Sushumna*, and are linked to nerve centres along the spinal cord. To check their locations at various points up the 'ladder', you can refer to the table of chakras on page 30.

Try standing upright and visualising the chakras within.

Meditating on the chakras

When you start meditating on the chakras, you will probably find some easier to sense than others. With practice, however, you should be able to feel them all.

If you find, after a few attempts at Chakra meditation (opposite), that you are having difficulty feeling the energy flow through certain chakras, it may be because the flow there is 'blocked'. Almost everyone will find one or more of their chakras blocked. However, you should not let blockages go untreated because they can create problems later on (see page 30 for a list of the chakras and the functions they govern).

Unblocking the chakras

If you suspect that one or more of your chakras are blocked, do not attempt to unblock them yourself. You should consult an appropriately qualified therapist as soon as possible, such as a practitioner of Ayurveda (see page 62). Ayurveda is an ancient Indian healing system that aims to restore health and balance to the mind and body through herbal remedies, diet, breathing exercises, purification, meditation, yoga postures, massage and other treatments.

A qualified Ayurvedic practitioner will be able to sense blockages in your chakras and can help to restore your natural energy flow.

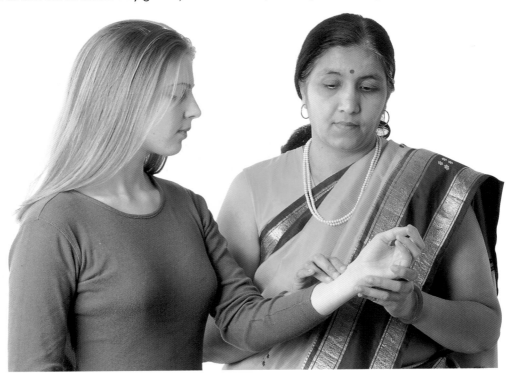

Chakra meditation

For this meditation, choose a quiet place where you will not be disturbed. Your clothing should be loose and comfortable. You may find it helps to close your eyes.

1 *Adopt the seated or cross-legged posture (see pages 14–15). Make sure that you are sitting upright with your spine straight and your head and spine in alignment. However, don't strain. Your posture should be comfortable and you should feel relaxed. Take three deep breaths, then breathe naturally.*

2 *Using your mind, try to sense the chakra at the base of your spine. You can imagine it as a lotus with the corresponding number of petals (see table on page 30), or as a spinning wheel or storehouse of energy. Choose the image that feels right for you, and sense the energy within it. What does it feel like to you?*

3 *Move your attention up to the next chakra in the lower abdomen, just above your genital area. Again feel the energy within it. Does the energy feel different compared to the energy of the base chakra?*

4 *If you have trouble feeling the energy flow in one or more of your chakras, try to 'breathe' energy into the affected area. In other words, as you inhale and exhale, imagine that your breath is revitalising the chakra concerned and filling it with life-giving energy.*

5 *Move your attention up through the other chakras, through the solar plexus or navel area, then the heart, then the throat, and up to the forehead, between the eyes. Feel the subtle differences of energy between the chakras as you move your attention through them. Finally, move your concentration to the top of your head and feel the chakra there. What does the energy feel like?*

6 *Gradually wind down your meditation, let your body relax even further, and then take a couple of deep breaths before finishing the exercise.*

Working through the chakras can help you to become more in tune with your energy.

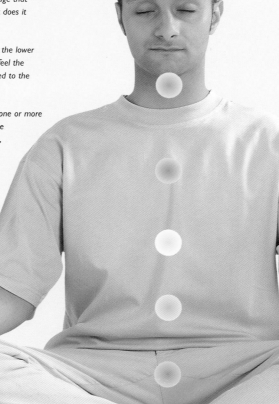

Visualisation

Visualisation is an extremely powerful technique that uses the imagination to create particular states of mind and being. It is becoming increasingly popular nowadays and can be used for a wide variety of purposes, such as improving the concentration and training the mind, or increasing self-confidence and problem-solving. It can even be used for healing or for helping to achieve spiritual enlightenment.

How visualisation works

Visualisation goes far beyond just the imagination. Although it uses the imagination to create mental images of things, it goes much further because it involves all the senses, and not just sight, smell, touch, hearing and taste, but the emotions as well. What's more, some visualisations can even manifest themselves on a physical level.

As an example of this, try to remember a situation that you found particularly frightening. It could be a terrifying car ride, for example, or a lonely walk late at night in a dark, secluded street. If you can't remember one, what about any phobias you might have? For example, if you are frightened of spiders, imagine one jumping onto your hand or into your hair. If you are afraid of heights, imagine jumping out of an aeroplane.

If you visualise this clearly enough, so that you can recall that past experience in detail, or feel the spider moving in your hair, you will

For some people, the very thought of spiders may elicit the same feelings and body sensations as seeing them in the flesh.

find that your body responds to this stress and you will notice some physical reactions taking place. For example, you will probably tense up and your pulse will get quicker. You might also find that you are breathing more rapidly. If the stress is strong enough, you might even find yourself sweating or shivering.

The reason your body is responding in this way is that our bodies do not distinguish between things we visualise and reality itself.

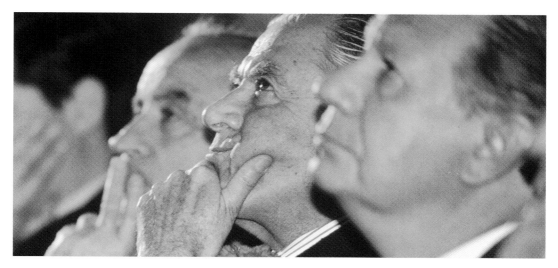

So if the situation you are visualising is stressful enough, it will trigger the body's 'fight or flight' mechanism (see page 16).

As we have already seen, when the fight or flight response kicks in, your body will shut down all the systems that are not essential to immediate survival, adrenaline and anti-inflammatory agents will be pumped into the system, and your body will be poised for potentially life-saving flight.

Benefits of visualisation

The good news about this is that you can use visualisation to achieve beneficial effects. For example, when we daydream about something that makes us happy, the brain produces endorphins and other pleasure-giving chemicals, and our bodies experience the physical sensations of joy. We can use visualisation to achieve the same effects.

A person nervous of public speaking may find visualising an attentive audience helpful.

If we now go back to our man with the fear of public speaking (see page 20), we can easily see how he could use visualisation to help himself over his fear. He could simply visualise himself in front of his audience, speaking confidently and clearly. The audience is smiling and hanging onto every word he says. He is enjoying himself and feeling very calm and comfortable. At the end of his speech, the audience applauds enthusiastically. If he keeps on visualising this situation in the same positive way, eventually the right side of his brain (see page 7) will come to associate the thought of public speaking with pleasure and he will find that his fear disappears.

So visualisation is not just all in the mind. Although it starts in the mind, it can have profoundly physical effects.

Making visualisation work for you

As mentioned earlier, visualisation can be hugely beneficial and can help you to achieve all kinds of things. If you want to conquer a fear, you can use visualisation to help you, as our man with the fear of public speaking could have done (see page 20). If you want to cure an addiction, perhaps to give up smoking, drinking or caffeine, or you would like to increase your self-confidence, you can use visualisation to help with that too.

The main thing to bear in mind with visualisation is that you should endeavour to do it as clearly and in as much detail as possible. You also need to keep doing it, in order to reinforce the message you are giving to the right side of your brain. This side of the

brain, you will recall, is the side that deals with feelings and intuition rather than thinking and speaking. It will receive your visualisations without question and transform them into feelings, once you get them past the left side of the brain (see page 7). Practice and repetition will help you achieve this.

Using the power of visualisation

Visualisation involves using two different kinds of imagery: active and receptive. Active imagery can be any image that is chosen and focused on for a particular purpose. Receptive imagery, on the other hand, involves allowing images to arise from the subconscious mind and following where they lead. Some people prefer the discipline of active imagery, while others feel more comfortable letting images surface in their own way. Some people feel comfortable using both types of imagery.

Whichever imagery you find you prefer, you can use either active or receptive images to help train the mind. If you would like to find out how easy or difficult it is for you to visualise something, and whether you prefer active or receptive imagery, try the 'Visualisation skills' exercise (opposite).

You can use visualisation skills to sharpen and focus your mind or for specific results, such as to unleash your creative potential.

Visualisation skills

This meditation is excellent for assessing and sharpening your powers of visualisation. Practise in a quiet place when you know you won't be disturbed.

1 *Adopt any posture that feels comfortable (see pages 14–15). The seated or cross-legged postures are best, but the lying down posture can also be used if you are not tired. Breathe naturally and close your eyes.*

2 *Try to visualise an oak leaf. What is it like? Try to see it in your mind's eye as though it really exists. See it in as much detail as you can. Notice everything about it: its colour, shape and texture. Notice every fine line on it. Turn the leaf over and study the other side. If you can bring in the other senses, so much the better. Rub the oak leaf between your fingers. What does it feel like? Can you hear the sound of your fingers rubbing the leaf? Put the leaf to your nose: can you smell it?*

3 *Open your eyes. Write down every sensation and detail. Repeat this exercise with the following objects: a coin, a rose and an ice-cream.*

Active or receptive?

What did you notice about each of the objects you have just visualised? Was the leaf vibrant or withered? Smooth or crumbly? What did you do with the coin? Was the rose hard to visualise? Could you taste the ice-cream? If you could only keep the object in view for a short time, you need to keep practising until you can hold each image for extended periods.

If you found you couldn't visualise these objects at all, don't worry: many people find visualisation hard but master it with practice. Alternatively, you may have found that your brain substituted different images, such as a dahlia instead of a rose. If so, you may be more comfortable with the flexibility of receptive imagery. Receptive images can be just as revealing as active ones, and both will help you to train your mind. Eventually, you should aim to be at ease with both types.

Writing down your experience can help you to see how best to use visualisation.

Increasing your understanding

Images are the language of your subconscious mind. If you can learn to communicate with your subconscious mind using and interpreting these images, you will have found a way to communicate with your subconscious and use the understanding it can bring. For example, if you want to understand other people or a situation you find confusing, you can ask your subconscious mind to help you. You will need to use receptive imagery to do this – in other words, you will need to let images arise freely.

So the next time you are in a situation you find difficult to understand, try the 'Gaining insight' experiment below.

Gaining insight

Try this technique to help you understand a particular feeling or situation.

1 Adopt the seated or cross-legged posture (see pages 14–15). Alternatively, you can do this meditation in the standing posture (see page 26). Relax into your chosen posture and breathe naturally for a few moments.

2 Close your eyes, and hold the feeling or situation you want to explore in your concentration for a few moments. When you are ready, ask your subconscious mind to produce an image that describes either the situation or the feeling that you are trying to understand.

Don't worry if the image that appears makes little sense at first; it may take you time to uncover the meaning of the animal, flower or other symbol your mind chooses.

3 Let the image surface. At first it may seem to have nothing to do with what you are asking. Persevere – it may take practice to understand the symbols of your mind. Perhaps your image is of a barking dog – then you realise the person you are trying to fathom is 'all bark and no bite'.

4 Once you have your image, and have studied it, close down the meditation and open your eyes. Think about the insights you have gained. You can continue to think about the image when you are not meditating.

Sacred space

Visualisation can help you to find a sacred space, a sanctuary you can go to in order to rest and receive comfort if you need it. If you also need to seek guidance, you can use visualisation to help you find a guide there.

There are many guided meditations to help you with this. Some are available on tape and talk you through the visualisation so that you can concentrate on responding to the imagery. In 'Sanctuary meditation' (below), you will need to use active and receptive imagery. When you have finished, think about what you saw or heard. It may take time before you fully understand it, or you may understand it immediately.

Sanctuary meditation

You can do this meditation whenever you like. Choose a quiet place where you will not be disturbed.

1 *Adopt the seated or cross-legged posture (see pages 14–15), whichever feels most comfortable to you. Once you have adopted your posture, take a few moments to relax into it and breathe naturally.*

2 *Close your eyes, and see yourself walking in a wood. You are following a small stream. You can hear the water flowing gently, trickling over rocks, and you can see patches of shining blue sky between the leaves of the trees. Squirrels run up the trunks of the trees in front of you. What colour are the squirrels? Birds are warbling in the branches over your head, and you can hear the crunch of twigs and leaves under your feet as you walk. You feel very comfortable, and very relaxed.*

3 *Up ahead, the trees part and you enter a large clearing. The stream flows through the clearing, and you can smell the heady scent of woodland flowers as you emerge into the glade. The clearing is peaceful, except for the sound of the water and occasional birdsong.*

4 *Lie down on the ground here, and relax totally. Soak in the warm sun. You are perfectly safe here and free to do as you wish. Stay here as long as you like, until you feel both rested and refreshed.*

5 *Now is the time, if you want to, to meet your guide. Relax, and wait for your guide to enter the glade from the trees on the far side. Your guide may be a man, a woman, or an animal. When you have greeted each other, pay special attention to anything your guide says. You can also use this time to ask questions on everyday or spiritual matters.*

6 *When you have finished, thank your guide and make your way out of the clearing, and into the wood. Gradually close down your meditation and come back to everyday consciousness. Open your eyes.*

If your guide didn't come to you this time, don't worry. Your guide will appear when the time is right.

Meditation for healing

An increasing number of doctors now believe that, in addition to having a well-balanced diet and taking enough physical exercise, practising meditation can lead to better health and improvements in our overall lifestyle and well-being.

How meditation helps

Meditation has wide-ranging benefits: it can help us to think more clearly and improve our energy levels so that we work more efficiently and tire less. It can help us to relax and create a distance from stressful situations so that we remain more in control and less overwhelmed by negative emotions. It can also help us to understand ourselves and to accept situations.

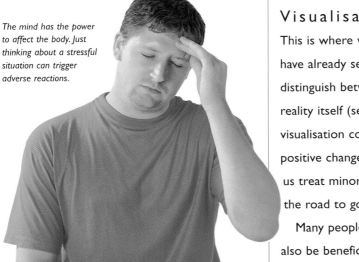

The mind has the power to affect the body. Just thinking about a stressful situation can trigger adverse reactions.

In addition to improving our quality of life and making us happier, the relaxation that meditation brings can help to improve our physical health. Positive thinking can encourage the production of endorphins and other 'feel-good' chemicals. We should never underestimate the mind's power to bring about change in the body, and we should try to think positively as much as possible.

Visualisation for healing

This is where visualisation comes in. As we have already seen, our bodies do not distinguish between things we visualise and reality itself (see page 34). So if we use visualisation correctly, it can bring about positive changes within the body that can help us treat minor ailments and put us back on the road to good health.

Many people believe that visualisation can also be beneficial in the treatment of more serious or long-standing complaints, but it must be emphasised that it should not be used to replace medical treatment: if you have a serious or persistent ailment, you should always consult a qualified medical practitioner. There is no reason, however, why you should not use visualisation alongside any medical treatment you are currently having. You could visualise, for example, a drug working more effectively, or you could see yourself feeling fit and radiant. Discuss your plans with your doctor first, to make sure that you are working together on this.

Current research

Research is still under way into the possible effects of meditation on our health but, as mentioned earlier, a growing number of conventional doctors are now recommending relaxation and meditation exercises to their patients in order to help them combat stress and stress-related illnesses (see page 5). Clinical studies continue, but in the meantime there is a growing belief that meditation

Many doctors are now recommending meditation and relaxation as an effective antidote to stress.

practice, alongside changes in diet and lifestyle, can help to do the following:

- Reduce migraines
- Combat insomnia
- Ease irritable bowel syndrome
- Soothe premenstrual syndrome
- Calm anxiety and reduce panic attacks
- Lower levels of stress hormones
- Improve circulation
- Regulate the pulse
- Lower blood pressure
- Control respiration
- Ease stomach cramps
- Aid digestion
- Ease depression
- Improve memory

*Deities from all religions are shown meditating,
illustrating its importance in spiritual
practice. However, meditation is also used to
aid mental, emotional and physical well-being.*

Personal development

In addition to its many physical health benefits,
meditation practice can also be of use in
psychotherapy, especially in those areas that
focus on personal development and self-
understanding. Through meditation, many
of us have learned that it is possible to
understand ourselves better and the nature of
our relationships with other people. With
regular practice, we can increase our
confidence and self-esteem, let go of past
hurts, and enjoy life more, both in our work
and in our social lives. We can learn how to
conquer fear and dispel doubts, and we can
transform that critical inner voice within us
into a valuable and supportive friend.

Using visualisation for healing

You don't have to wait until you feel ill to do healing visualisations. In fact, it is often a good idea to do it when you are feeling well. Good health needs to be protected and, in addition to a balanced, healthy diet and plenty of exercise and restful sleep, visualisation can help you to maintain your good health and guard against illness and disease. It can also help you to become more in touch with your body and physical changes. The 'Healing the body' exercise (below) can be used to heal part of the body or to maintain good health.

Healing the body

This exercise is excellent for purifying and healing and for revitalising the whole body. Make sure that your clothing is loose and comfortable before you start the exercise.

1   *Adopt the seated or lying down posture (see pages 14–15), whichever feels most comfortable to you. If necessary, you can also do this visualisation while you are standing or walking (see page 26).*

2   *Allow your body to relax and breathe naturally. If you are not walking, you can close your eyes if it helps you to concentrate.*

3   *Check over your body and release any tension that you are holding. Start with the top of your head, then move your attention down to your forehead. Relax your eyebrows and eyelids, your ears, nostrils, mouth and jaw, then your neck, shoulders, arms and hands. Shift your concentration to your chest and heart, then your stomach, abdomen, buttocks and genitals, and finally your legs and feet.*

4   *When you are relaxed, begin the healing. Imagine you are standing under a shower of whiteish-blue light. The light comes in through the top of your head, then washes through your body, clearing it of impurities. Feel the light wash through your head and into your neck, outwards through the shoulders until it fills your arms and hands. Let the light continue down through your chest, back, and torso, and down through your legs and into your feet. Feel the light taking out all the impurities and toxins from your body, and if there are any parts of your body that need special healing, focus on them and let the light purify them. Let the light do this until you feel that your whole body has been cleansed. You may need to do this several times before you feel completely purified.*

5   *When the light has cleansed and purified you, let it take the impurities from your body out through the soles of your feet and into the earth beneath you, where they are cleansed until they disappear.*

6   *Now that the impurities have gone, let the light flow back up through your feet and into your body, charging it with vibrant, healing energy. Feel it rush up your legs and torso, setting the whole length of your spine tingling. Feel it flow into your heart and chest, outwards into your arms and hands, and up into your shoulders and neck. Finally, let it flood up into your face to the top of your head. If any parts of your body need special healing, let the vibrant light flow in and heal them. Hold the image of your whole body flooded with healing light, then let the light ascend up through the top of your head and out into the universe.*

7   *Give yourself a few moments to relax and take a few deep, smooth breaths. When you are ready, close the meditation and open your eyes.*

Note

If you find the whiteish-blue light hard to visualise, imagine pure water instead, such as water from a healing spa, or anything else that signifies a purifying force to you. If you are religious, you can visualise holy water or the healing breath of a deity.

Colour and light

The powers of colour and light can have a great influence on us and on many aspects of our daily lives. Colours can affect our moods and are associated with particular emotions: red, for instance, is often linked with anger, blue with peace and relaxation, and yellow with mental clarity. We also attribute different qualities to colours: for example, we associate wealth and abundance with gold. Light is also very powerful: it can affect our moods, how things appear, and how we view things around us.

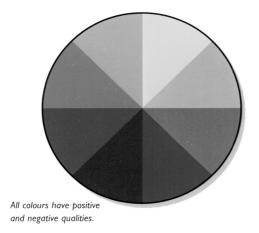

All colours have positive and negative qualities.

The power of colour

It is important to have a healthy balance of all the colours in your life. If one colour is missing, it could represent an aspect of your life that you find difficult to accept. For example, if there is an absence of blue in your wardrobe and home, you could be having problems with communication and with creativity. Likewise, if you have an excess of a particular colour, the energy associated with that colour may be dominating your life.

at the expense of other energies. You can use colours to energise your body and spirit and to create balance in your surroundings. You can also use them for healing, by utilising their special qualities. Interpretations of colour energies vary between people, cultures, therapies and religions, but here the chart opposite shows some of the most popular interpretations from around the world.

Both the colour of gold and the metal itself are associated with wealth.

Colours and their attributes

Colour	In balance	Out of balance
Red	The material world, status in life, survival, courage, physical strength and vitality	Greed, anger, cruelty, vulgarity, violence
Pink	Empathy, warmth, stimulation and loyalty	Selfishness, fickleness and egotism
Orange	Sexual energy, sensuality, happiness, optimism and friendship	Loss of sexual energy or obsession with sex, and fatigue and pessimism
Yellow	Self-esteem, willpower, determination, confidence, inner power, mental energy, intellect and mental alertness	Lack of mental clarity and concentration, stubbornness, inflexibility and deviousness
Green	Emotions, including love and sympathy, relationships, harmony, freedom, growth and renewal	Jealousy, possessiveness, insecurity, dislike of change, dwelling on the past
Turquoise	Healing, eloquence and self-expression, independence and protection	Allergies and other immune system disorders, tendency to be easily influenced, restricted self-expression, and vulnerability
Blue	Communication, creativity, inspiration, expression, peace, trust, devotion, sincerity and relaxation	Insincerity, suspicion, distrust, sadness and inability to communicate
Indigo	Imagination, intuition, clarity of thought, dreams, mystery and secrecy	Paranoia, nightmares, confusion and deceit
Violet	Understanding, higher consciousness, spiritual development, link with the divine, idealism, reverence and commitment	Misunderstanding and misinterpretation, fanaticism, domination, adherence to outmoded beliefs, and lack of faith
Silver	Clairvoyance, the subconscious mind, fluidity and transformation	Suggestibility and lack of stability
Gold	Wealth, abundance, spirituality, higher ideals, pleasure and leisure	Avarice, poverty, apathy, laziness and excessive pleasure-seeking
White	Order, completion, clarity, purity, wholeness, simplicity and innocence	Rigidity, extremism, obsessive cleanliness, puritanism and naivety
Brown	Stability and centredness, resourceful and nurturing	Depression, dullness and inability to change
Black	Deep power, self-knowledge, discernment and judgement	Tyranny, prejudice, blindness and refusal to compromise

Finding the right balance

As you will see from the chart just shown, it is possible to have too much of a colour or not enough of it. Meditation will help you to harmonise these colour energies in your life.

The Exploring colour meditation (below) will help you to become familiar with different colour energies. You can also take it a step further and explore your own feelings about each colour as its energies emerge.

Exploring further

You can build on the meditation below by using different shades of a colour. For example, if your blue is pale this time, next time imagine a deeper or darker blue. Try to spot changes in their energies and note your feelings about them. Noting your feelings is useful because some colours may have different qualities for you than the ones described in the table (see page 45).

Exploring colour

This exercise is very good for improving your concentration and mental focus. It will also give you an insight into the different energies of different colours and what those energies mean to you as an individual.

1 Adopt a seated or cross-legged posture (see pages 14–15) or a standing posture (see page 26).

2 Breathe naturally and, if it helps you to concentrate, close your eyes.

3 Think of the colour red. Visualise a red bubble of energy all around you. Feel the red bubble expanding and contracting as you breathe in and out How does the energy feel? Does the red feel light, dark, bright or dull?

4 Now think of the colour pink. Once again, visualise yourself inside a pink bubble. What shade of pink is your bubble? What feelings does it trigger? How does the energy feel?

5 Now do the same with the following colours: orange, yellow, green, turquoise, indigo, violet, silver, gold, white, brown and black.

6 When you have finished, close down the meditation. Note any feelings you had about the colours and their energies, particularly any strong likes or dislikes you experienced.

As you focus on each colour and chakra, be aware of any feelings they evoke within you.

Using colour to solve your problems

Attributing colours to people or situations can help you understand them better. For example, if you are having trouble with a colleague, visualise the person and ask your subconscious for a colour to describe that person. If green arises, consider if there is jealousy between you. Once you see what energies are at work, you will be able to improve things.

Colour and the chakras

Meditating on different colours and the seven main chakras is a useful way of strengthening your visualisation skills and discovering the power of your chakras.

As mentioned earlier, each chakra is associated with a particular colour and energy quality (see page 30). You can explore these energies and help to unlock them using the 'Chakra colour meditation'.

Chakra colour meditation

Use this meditation to help you energise the chakras and identify with their different qualities and associated colours.

1   Adopt a seated or cross-legged posture (see pages 14–15). Make sure that you are sitting upright with your back straight and your head and spine in alignment. Relax and breathe naturally.

2   Visualise the first chakra at the base of your spine. Imagine the colour red flowing into that area: sense the energy of this powerful colour revitalising your chakra. What does it feel like?

3   Move your attention up to the next chakra, the sacral chakra in the lower abdomen, just above your genital area. Visualise vibrant orange flowing into this area and feel it energising the chakra. Does the energy feel different from the energy of the base chakra?

4   Work your way up through the other chakras, using yellow in the solar plexus or navel area, then green at the heart, blue at the throat, indigo between the eyes and then violet on the top of your head. How do all the energies differ from one another?

5   When you have finished, take a couple of deep breaths and gradually close down your visualisation. Open your eyes.

Visualising your chakras and the colours associated with them can be a very powerful practice.

Meditating on the power of light

Visualising light in your meditation is a very powerful way of utilising its special qualities. Light can be very energising and healing, as we have already seen in the 'Golden flower meditation' (see page 26) and the 'Healing the body' meditation (see pages 42–43).

You can meditate on light in other ways too. For example, meditating on the sunlight is very uplifting and can also help treat seasonal affective disorder syndrome (SADS), or 'winter blues'. This condition is believed to be caused by light deprivation, which occurs especially in winter or if a person has spent long periods of time in a dark or shady place.

Using different coloured lights in meditation will unlock different energies. If you would like to try this for yourself, simply do the chakra

Focusing on the flame of a candle can clear your mind.

colour meditation (see page 47), but instead of visualising each coloured energy, visualise light in the appropriate colour for that chakra instead. So for the base chakra you would visualise red light, for the sacral chakra you would visualise orange light, and so on.

You can also meditate on light to improve your concentration. The 'Candle meditation' (see opposite) is a simple exercise that will still the mind and bring peace and relaxation.

Different coloured lights can unlock different energies when used in meditation.

Candle meditation

For this exercise you will need a quiet, darkened room and a lit candle. A simple white or cream candle is best.

1 Adopt either a seated, cross-legged or kneeling posture (see pages 14–15). Choose whichever posture you find most comfortable to sustain for a reasonable period of time. Place the lit candle in front of you.

2 Relax, breathe naturally, and focus your gaze on the flame. Empty your mind of all thoughts and just concentrate on the flame. Don't stare: just gaze softly at the flame and allow your eyes to blink when necessary. Let your mind slow down to a receptive, alpha state (see page 7). Whenever your mind tries to sidetrack you with other thoughts, bring it gently but firmly back to the flame.

3 Keep up this exercise for as long as is comfortable, then gradually close down the meditation.

Note that this well-known exercise is primarily intended to help you build up concentration and mental focus. However, you can also adapt it to help you develop other qualities. For example, you can also use a candle of a particular colour if you want to explore a specific energy. Perhaps you might like to use a green candle to help you reconnect with feelings of love and harmony after an argument (see page 45 for the colours and their energies). You can also use this exercise to sharpen your visualisation skills: close your eyes at the end of step 2 and try to see the candle in your mind's eye, in as much detail as possible. Then close the visualisation.

The flickering flame of a candle gives the restless mind something to focus on. This helps you to quieten the inner chatter and develop your concentration skills.

The power of sound

Towards the end of the nineteenth century, American doctors discovered that some types of music could stimulate blood flow. Since then, there has been increased medical interest in the therapeutic qualities of sound.

How sound affects us

Just as colour and light can influence our moods, sound has the power to affect our emotions. It can reach deep inside us and alter the way we feel and even the way we react in a given situation. Sound is made up of waves of pressure that resonate at different frequencies. These different levels of sound affect us in different ways. For example, a high-pitched sound, such as a scream, will set our nerves on edge and make us tense, whereas the gentle sound of water trickling from a fountain will soothe and relax us. In the same way, gentle, beautiful music is calming and can inspire creativity, whereas loud, thudding music is irritating and will leave us feeling stressed. In extreme cases, very loud music can even cause headache and damage the hearing.

There are exceptions to this. There are times, for instance, when irritating or chaotic sounds can energise us or inspire our creativity. For example, the bewitching sounds of Ravel's concerto 'Bolero' were inspired by the interminable sawing rhythm of a mill.

However, these cases are very much the exceptions, and it is better to try to improve the quality of sound around us whenever possible so that we can become more relaxed and avoid increasing the amount of unnecessary stress in our lives. This helps us to function more efficiently and enjoy a better quality of life and a greater level of happiness.

People are drawn to waterfalls because the sound of running water has a soothing effect.

Classical music tends to have a soothing and even inspirational effect on the mind.

Sound as healer

Research is still under way into the therapeutic potential of sound, but there is a growing belief that certain sound waves can affect the pulse, respiration and blood pressure, and improve mental clarity. Sound therapists now use machines to send healing sound waves to ailing parts of the body, and to help autistic patients to hear properly.

Research in both the US and Europe during the 1980s and 1990s showed that music could be used to reduce stress levels and help patients to recover from illnesses more quickly. Music therapists are increasingly being asked to help treat patients with learning difficulties and other mental and physical disabilities. They use music to encourage patients to find ways of expressing themselves and even to give pain relief.

Using the qualities of sound

There are many ways to use sound in your meditation practice. For example, you can have beautiful music playing in the background. I have found that instrumental pieces work best for this, and would recommend gentle classical or New Age music. Sounds of nature, such as sounds of the seashore, also create the right atmosphere. Whichever sounds you choose, try meditating on each sound with mindfulness (see page 18). In other words, be aware of every sound as it happens. In this way, your appreciation of the sounds will be intense.

Using sound to solve your problems

Like colour (see page 47), sound can help you to understand people or situations. If you are finding it hard to understand someone, hold that person in your mind's eye and ask your subconscious to describe him or her with a sound. If it's a whisper, it could suggest the person is timid or unsure. If it's a roar, then perhaps the person is overbearing or insensitive. The sound and your interpretation of it give an indication of your feelings and put you in a better position to improve your relationship.

Sound within the body

Chants or mantras (see page 24) help to still the mind and create a sense of tranquillity and peace. The vibrations are felt throughout the body and can lead to a state of bliss and euphoria. Experiment with a few sounds and mantras and feel the effects different sound vibrations have within your body.

The 'Chakra sound meditation' links sound vibrations with the seven main chakras (see page 28). Like the 'Chakra colour meditation' (see page 47), this will help you identify with your chakras and unlock their power.

Chakra sound meditation

This meditation is best performed in a silent place where no other sounds will be able to disturb your concentration.

1 Adopt a seated or cross-legged posture (see pages 14–15). Relax and breathe naturally. Visualise the chakra at the base of your spine. Make a long sound 'DOH' in as low a key as you can. Imagine the 'DOH' is coming from the chakra itself. Let it vibrate for 10 seconds at least. What does it feel like?

2 Move your attention to the sacral chakra in the lower abdomen. Make a long sound 'RAY', in a slightly higher key. Hold it for at least 10 seconds, and try to imagine it coming from the chakra itself. How does the energy of this sound differ from the energy of the 'DOH'?

Practising chanting with other people can intensify the power of the sounds.

3 Shift your attention to the solar plexus or navel area, and make a long sound 'MI', as in 'see', in a slightly higher key than the 'RAY'. Again, and throughout the meditation, hold the sound for at least 10 seconds. How does it feel?

4 Now focus on the heart chakra, and make a long sound 'FAH', as in 'far'. Sound it in a slightly higher key than the 'MI'. Feel the vibrations coming from your heart area. How does this energy feel?

5 Now, do the same for the throat chakra, using the sound 'SOH' in a slightly higher key. Can you feel the differences in energy as the tones become higher?

6 Shift your attention to the chakra on your forehead, and make a long sound 'LAH' in a slightly higher key. Then move your focus to the crown chakra and make the sound 'TI', as in 'tee'. This should be the highest pitched sound of all. How does it feel?

7 Finally, be absolutely still. Hear the sounds your body makes from within. Pay special attention to them, because they will help you to forge greater awareness of your body. Then, breathe deeply and close the meditation.

Note
You can use any sounds of your choice for this as long as they are of one syllable, resonate in the body, and get progressively higher as you work up the chakras.

Using fragrances in meditation

Since ancient times we have been aware of the emotive power of fragrances. We have used incense and fragrant oils in our rituals for thousands of years. They have the power to change our mood and can evoke images and memories of places far away.

How fragrances affect us

Your sense of smell is very sensitive and acts as an early warning system that helps you to detect threats to your safety. For example, if there is smoke in your home, your nose alerts you so that you can check for fire.

What happens is that the nose detects a smell, and then the mind associates it with an image or idea. So if the nose detects smoke,

Smell is the most evocative of the senses. A simple aroma, such as a lemon or perfume, can instantly conjure up an image of a special place or person.

the brain will associate it with fire and burning. This link between the nose detecting a smell and then the brain producing an image in response to it is what gives smells their power to inspire the imagination.

The physical effects of fragrances

What we smell can also affect the body. This is because, as already mentioned, our bodies do not distinguish between things we visualise and reality itself (see page 34). If we think about something that makes us happy, the brain produces pleasure-giving chemicals, and we feel physical sensations of joy (see page 35).

In this way, what we smell can affect us physically. The smell is detected in the nose, then interpreted by the brain, which produces an image or idea, and that idea triggers a response in the body. We should therefore not underestimate the powerful effects that scents can have on us. They can lift our moods or depress us, comfort us or irritate us.

Healing fragrances

Since what we smell can affect us physically, it is not surprising that we have used fragrances in healing since ancient times. The art of aromatherapy has in fact been practised for thousands of years. The earliest record of its use was in China in 4,500 BC. The Ancient Egyptians also used essential oils, both for therapeutic purposes and for embalming.

In Ancient Greece, the great physician Hippocrates (460–377 BC), known as the 'father of medicine', used aromatic herbs and spices to treat his patients, and later the Greek surgeon Galen (AD 130–AD 201) used essential oils (see page 62) in his work. These essential oils, or aromatic liquids, were usually obtained from plants.

In medieval Europe, herbs were often used to help

Hippocrates used medicinal herbs to treat the sick.

fight disease, and in Renaissance England, Queen Elizabeth I (1533–1603) supported the use of aromatic herbs, spices and oils.

Since then, a variety of European chemists have published studies on the therapeutic uses of essential oils, and today aromatherapy is becoming an increasingly popular way of treating ailments and maintaining good health.

The aromas of different herbs and flowers can have strong effects on our moods and well-being.

Herbal oils have been used therapeutically for thousands of years, and aromatherapy is now a widely used therapy.

Using the power of fragrances

You can use fragrances in your meditation in many ways. Incense, for example, can help to create the right atmosphere for your meditation. Choose incense sticks, smudge sticks or burn incense on charcoal in an incense burner. You can also burn essential oils in an oil burner: just fill the reservoir with water, add a few drops of your chosen oil, and then light the candle underneath and it will fill your meditation space with your chosen fragrance. All of these are available from New Age or natural health shops.

Used in many religious ceremonies, incense can help to open the mind for meditation.

Burning an essential oil while you do a 'Healing the body' meditation (see pages 42–43) is a very powerful way of using fragrances to heal the body and the mind. You could also add a few drops to your bath and perform a healing meditation while you soak.

The table opposite lists some of the main essential oils and their helpful qualities in relation to meditation. Bear in mind that these essential oils are very strong and some are not suitable for children, pregnant women, breastfeeding mothers, convalescents, or anyone suffering from a serious illness. If you are in any doubt, consult a qualified aromatherapist first.

Aromatherapy oils can create an atmosphere conducive to meditation or relaxation.

Many aromatic herbs, such as ylang ylang and bergamot, have medicinal properties.

Essential oils and their healing qualities

Essential oil	Action	Healing qualities
Bergamot	Uplifting, refreshing, calming, energising and revitalising	Eases stress, restores appetite, and soothes anxiety and depression
Cypress	Purifying, soothing and invigorating	Calms the nervous system and helps ease menopausal symptoms, hay fever and stress
Geranium	Uplifting and balancing	Soothes premenstrual tension and depression, calms the nervous system and lifts the spirits
Ginger	Warming, circulating, relaxing and has anticatarrhal properties	Helps prevent and ease travel sickness and nausea, stimulates the immune system against colds, helps to clear catarrh, calms the digestive system and improves circulation
Grapefruit	Relaxing, purifying, uplifting and emotionally balancing	Helps to regulate the emotions, eases stress and anger, and helps treat colds and respiration problems
Juniper	Purifying, stimulating, uplifting, reassuring and soothing	Helps to clear the mind and aid concentration, eases aches and pains, and soothes the mind and body
Lavender	Relaxing, soothing, cheering, balancing, cleansing and harmonising	Helps to ease high blood pressure, stress and tension headaches, and is particularly soothing for women after childbirth
Lemon	Purifying, refreshing and stimulating	Reduces mental exhaustion, eases stress, stimulates concentration and improves circulation
Orange	Relaxing and soothing	Helps prevent travel sickness, aids digestion, and eases stress and tension headaches
Sandalwood	Purifying, relaxing, balancing, aphrodisiac and decongestant	Calms the nervous system, helps to ease emotional problems, has a balancing effect on the mind, body and spirit, and also calms the mind in preparation for meditation practice
Ylang ylang	Calming, uplifting, balancing, purifying, invigorating and aphrodisiac	Helpful for sexual problems, prevents hyperventilation, soothes anxiety, helps regulate pulse, reduces panic attacks and eases depression

Meditations for stressful situations

Sometimes, even with careful planning, life can become hectic or stressful. Traffic delays, unexpected calls and unforeseen events can all play havoc with our daily lives. Problems may arise and may seem insurmountable. At times like these, when all you can do is watch your peace of mind go out the window, try these quick meditations.

Travelling meditation

This meditation is particularly good for relieving stress when you are running late. It can be performed anywhere: on a train, on a bus, in a traffic jam, but for safety's sake make sure you're not driving while you do it!

1 *Let the whole of your body go loose, relaxing any areas of tension, and take a couple of deep breaths.*

2 *Accept that you have now done all you can to make up the lost time. There is nothing more you can do to make you get there any faster.*

3 *Focus on your breathing, and visualise the anxiety or worry simply floating away with each exhalation. Don't follow it, just let it go.*

4 *Each time the anxiety tries to come back, gently silence it and bring your mind back to its inner calm and peace. If the chatter persists, try repeating the mantra 'PEACE' with each exhalation.*

Visualisation can transport your mind to the most tranquil of scenes in an instant.

Step at a time

This meditation provides quick relief if you feel overwhelmed by too many things to do. In the longer term, you should try to lighten your load (see page 10) and prioritise remaining tasks.

1 Stop what you are doing and take a few seconds to relax yourself. Release the tension from your body and breathe naturally.

2 Accept that you can't do everything at once. You can only do one thing at a time. Decide to focus on just one task, and clear your mind of everything else. Whenever your mind tries to think of other things still to be done, gently bring it back to the task in hand.

3 Now focus on that one task with mindfulness (see page 18). Be aware of everything about it and use all your senses as much as possible: sight, smell, touch and so on. Calmly watch yourself doing it until the job is done. Then move on and complete the next task.

Seeing the bigger picture

This visualisation is a good one to try if you find yourself in a particularly frustrating or stressful situation. It will help you to be aware of the bigger picture and put your problems into perspective. After a little practice you should be able to do the whole thing in just a few seconds.

1 Take a few moments to stop and be aware of yourself. Then become aware of everything else around you.

2 As you do this, let your awareness expand so that you can feel everything happening within a couple of kilometres or miles around you. Try to see everything: people travelling on buses, walking into buildings, or working in fields – wherever you are, let your mind become aware of it.

3 Gradually expand the picture that you see in your mind's eye so that you can take in the whole country. Imagine people going about their daily lives in the north and south, west and east, and in all the towns and cities.

4 Let your awareness expand further, until your country becomes a shape on the globe that is Earth. See the planet moving through space. Notice the tiny continents and seas on its surface. Be aware that you are there, but that you are so small that you have become invisible from this vantage point.

5 Whatever has been worrying you should now feel really small in comparison to this view of the planet. Try to keep that perspective as you zero back in on yourself: tell yourself that this situation is really very small and that you will be able to handle it.

Expanding your awareness of the world can help you to put problems into perspective.

Bubble of protection

If ever you feel vulnerable, intimidated, or just in need of protection in some way, try this visualisation. It will help you to distance yourself from the source of the worry and make you feel safe and protected.

1 *Shake out all the tension from your body, allow yourself to relax in whatever position you are in. Breathe naturally.*

2 *Imagine a bubble of blue-white light all around you. You are safe inside it. The bubble is charged with sparkling, protective energy. It moves with you, and although it is soft on the inside, on the outside it is strong and is shielding you from whatever is making you anxious. It is keeping whatever is worrying you at a distance.*

3 *While you are inside the bubble, focus on your breathing. Visualise the blue-white light flowing in and out of your pores as you inhale and exhale. The sparkling light is filling you with strength and energy.*

4 *Keep the bubble around you until the pressure is over and you feel comfortable enough to let it go.*

Boost your confidence

This visualisation will help you to face difficult situations calmly, so if you need to soothe your nerves and boost your self-confidence, perhaps for a job interview or before speaking in public, this meditation is for you.

1 *Take a few moments to release all the tension from your body. Take a couple of deep breaths, then breathe naturally again.*

2 *Visualise yourself entering into the challenging situation with confidence. If it is a job interview or a public speech, for instance, see yourself walking in and exuding self-confidence. You are very relaxed and talking freely and confidently with the interviewer or the audience. The exchange between you is very positive, and the interviewer or audience looks enthusiastic when you are speaking. You answer all questions happily and with confidence. At the end, the interviewer or audience shows a lot of enthusiasm for what you have said and you feel happy that your performance has been so impressive.*

3 *Keep this image in your mind as long as possible. To reinforce the visualisation, try repeating a positive affirmation, something like 'I can handle this' or 'I am supremely confident' (see page 20).*

Note

You can also do this meditation to help you get over exam nerves. Replace step 2 as follows:

Visualise yourself feeling very at ease about the exam and speaking or writing the answers very confidently. You are relaxed and happy, and speaking or writing smoothly and comfortably. At the end, see yourself feeling extremely pleased with what you have done and confident that you are going to pass.

When you are nervous, take a few minutes to visualise some new self-confidence.

Glossary

Adrenaline
A hormone that prepares the body for the 'fight or flight' response. When it is released into the system by the adrenal gland, it has widespread effects on the muscles, circulation and sugar metabolism. The heartbeat quickens, breathing becomes more rapid and shallow, and the metabolic rate increases.

Affirmation
A statement that you can repeat silently or out loud to yourself until the constant repetition becomes meaningless and you are aware only of the sound of the affirmation in your head. Repeating affirmations helps to still the mind, and can get messages through to the right side of the brain, which deals with feelings and intuition. When the affirmation reaches the right side of the brain and is transformed into feeling, it can have a great influence on the mind, body and overall well-being.

Alpha state
This is when the brain emits slower electrical patterns, which are called 'alpha' waves. In the alpha state we are less active and more receptive and open to our feelings. The alpha state is most likely to happen when we let ourselves live in the present moment rather than in the future or the past.

Aromatherapy
A system of healing based on treating ailments using essential plant oils. Methods include massage with essential oils, adding oils to bath water or burning oils in a room.

Ayurveda
An Indian healing system that aims to restore health and balance to the body through herbal remedies, diet, breathing exercises, purification, yoga postures and massage.

Beta state
This is when the brain emits faster electrical patterns, which are called 'beta' waves. In this state we are able to rationalise, analyse and think about the past and future. We are usually in a beta state when we are awake and in a busy, thinking state of mind.

Chakras
Energy centres in the body. These spinning wheels of spiritual energy keep our bodies and spirits in balance and store the invisible life force that Indian yogis call *prana*, the Chinese call *ch'i* and the Japanese call *ki*.

Ch'i
The invisible life force that permeates everything; it surrounds everything and is within all things. Indian yogis call it *prana* and the Japanese call it *ki*.

Endorphins
Chemical compounds derived from a substance in the pituitary gland. They have pain-relieving properties and are responsible for sensations of pleasure. They are sometimes known as 'happy chemicals'.

Essential oils
These are aromatic liquids that are usually obtained by distilling or expressing them from parts of plants. They are very powerful and can be used for healing and to help create particular states of mind.

Kundalini
A dormant energy stored in the base chakra, which yogis aim to reactivate and send upwards through the other chakras.

Mantra

A sound, word or statement that you can repeat to yourself. The sound qualities of a mantra are important, and can resonate through the body to bring about a transformation of consciousness. Some people believe that mantras possess magical power.

Mindfulness

A state of mind where you are fully aware of everything in the present moment. It heightens sensitivity and enables us to feel things more intensely. It also helps us to be more aware and observant and perform tasks more efficiently.

Music therapy

A system of natural healing where patients are encouraged to listen to music to ease their pain and anxiety, and to promote recovery from a wide range of ailments.

Prana

The invisible universal life force energy that permeates everything. The Chinese call this energy *ch'i* and the Japanese call it *ki*.

Seasonal Affective Disorder Syndrome (SADS)

A disorder in which a person's mood is said to change according to the season of the year. During winter there is depression, slowing of the mind and body, and excessive eating and sleeping. With the arrival of spring the symptoms subside. Exposure to additional light during the day is believed to ease the symptoms. SADS is not yet a clinically accepted condition.

Sound therapy

A system of healing in which practitioners work with the voice or with electronic or musical instruments to generate sound waves that are believed to restore balance to the body and encourage healing.

Sushumna

A central channel in the body. The seven main chakras ascend up this channel and are linked to nerve centres along the spinal cord.

Index

Picture credits

Corbis: pps 4, 18, 35, 51, 55, 59.